"John Bull"

BOOK OF PITFALLS

BY MAJOR GENERAL

SIR WYNDHAM CHILDS

K.C.M.G., K.B.E., C.B.

JOHN BULL'S
BOOK OF PITFALLS

BY MAJOR-GENERAL SIR WYNDHAM CHILDS
K.C.M.G., K.B.E., C.B.

CONTENTS

INTRODUCTION

TO those who read this formidable list it must at once occur that the criminal law should, in some cases at any rate, make such things impossible.

I want to explain, in a few words, why it is that the police are frequently unable to take any action and why it is vital that readers of " John Bull " should protect themselves and their fellow-countrymen through the medium of that journal and of the Investigation Department which I direct.

Firstly, in many cases there is not sufficient evidence in the " police court sense " to prove fraudulent intention and, in others, people who have been victimised do not like it to be known. They will not go to the police or give evidence. Again, there is the difficulty of attending courts to give evidence for example, a man living at John o' Groats may have been swindled by a man in London. It would be necessary for the victim to come all the way to London, to remain there whilst the case was on remand before the magistrate, and again to attend at the Old Bailey or the Central Criminal Court if the case were committed for trial. All this means loss of time and money and the game is not worth the candle.

There is an alternative, however. Publicity properly and truthfully utilised without exaggeration or malice, and in the public interest, will kill a fraud quicker than any police proceedings, which, of their very nature, must be lengthy.

After some years, I now feel in the happy position that, scattered all over the United Kingdom—and, indeed, I can say almost all over the world—are a body of readers of " John Bull " who write to me, not only when they have been swindled, but when they are suspicious ; and I can say without any exaggeration whatever, that no fraud can be even started without my getting letters from readers expressing their suspicions, which are almost invariably well founded.

To those who read this brochure, I would say that if you wish to help your fellow-men and discover anything of the same type, write to me at once in order that the matter may be immediately investigated and the hammer blow of publicity be speedily delivered.

" JOHN BULL,"
93, LONG ACRE,
LONDON, W.C.2.

JOHN BULL'S
BOOK OF PITFALLS

CHAPTER I.

PITFALLS EVERY HOUSEWIFE SHOULD AVOID

THE door-to-door (frequently the back door !) type of canvasser is undoubtedly the most predatory of his species. I use the word " predatory " advisedly, as depicting a denizen of the jungle who emerges, seizes his victim and once more disappears.

The canvasser usually arrives at a time when the husband is at work and the wife busy with her household duties. Such is his insistence that it is a fact that lots of women will sign anything without reading it, in order to get rid of the nuisance.

THE TEA TRICK.

At the moment a small army of canvassers is engaged in working the tea trick throughout the country.

Housewives are persuaded to buy a pound of tea a week, usually at an exaggerated price a pound, for a period of eight weeks. This, it is stated, entitles the buyer to participate in the wonderful profit-sharing scheme and a cash gift of £3 is promised " in a very reasonable period." The period, of course, is not stated, and therein lies the snag.

In one case which came to my notice, after months of delay and several visits to the firm's offices, a woman eventually obtained 20s., and since then her name has been used continuously, much to her annoyance, as if she had been a recent cash winner.

Dozens of housewives are being bluffed by canvassers into buying cheap tea at a dear price without realising until too late the tricky conditions of the £3 gift offer.

ADVICE.—Buy your tea at a reputable shop and have nothing to do with people who make, at your door, offers of this description.

THE LEFT PARCEL TRICK.

An individual arrives at a house with a parcel bearing the address. The wife, under the impression that the parcel contains something ordered by a member of her family, signs for the goods.

A few weeks later a collector approaches with a bill (*e.g.*, a bedspread valued 11/- contained in the hitherto unopened package). Protests that the goods had never been ordered are of no avail and eventually County Court proceedings follow and judgment with costs is obtained.

ADVICE.—Never sign your name to anything without reading what you are signing. Don't take any goods into your house unless you are perfectly satisfied that they are intended for some member of your household and have, in fact, been ordered by him or her.

THE LEFT-OVER LINO DODGE.

Respectable-looking men wearing white aprons call on a householder and ask whether she would like to acquire a real bargain. They give the name of some famous firm and pretend that they have just finished a job at some local house, that they were left with an odd length of linoleum and do not desire to have the trouble of carrying it all the way back to London, so they had telephoned to their employers, who had authorised them to sell the remainder for £3.

After their departure and a further and more careful inspection of the linoleum it is discovered that it is of very inferior quality and not worth half the amount paid.

Representation to the firm discloses the fact that the men are impostors.

Advice.—Don't buy things at the door without a thorough inspection of their quality. If you don't understand enough about the matter, don't take any risk or waste your money. Shoddy goods are easy to produce and difficult to detect as such, unless you are an expert.

THE SALVAGE GOODS SALE FRAUD.

A printed circular is left by a traveller for the perusal of a housewife with the information that one of the firm's travellers will call in a few days to submit samples. A great clearance sale is announced of salvage goods which are offered at bargain prices. All the goods mentioned are of a nature calculated to appeal to every housewife. There are towels, glass-cloths, dusters, serviettes, handkerchiefs, stockings and rugs and sometimes also furs and costumes.

In due course a polite salesman arrives and assures the householder that his firm, which has headquarters in London and branches in the provinces, gives its assurance that all the goods will be equal to sample.

Purchasers are further protected, it is pointed out, by the fact that no payment is required until delivery, which is promised within twenty-one days.

But having enthused a customer in this way the salesman uses all his wiles to persuade her to " snap up " some other bargains which he happens to have with him.

It is rarely that he fails to effect a cash sale of some sort, but the goods thus sold usually prove unsatisfactory.

The promised bargains never arrive, and if protest is made to the " headquarters " of the firm at *e.g.* London, Manchester or Leeds, the letter inevitably comes back inscribed " Unknown."

In one case which came before my notice a reader paid £3 3s. od. for a suit length on the understanding that a tailor would call to measure him and that a suit would be made without further charge. No one ever called and letters to the alleged firm have all been returned marked " Unknown."

ADVICE.—Don't buy " bargains " on the doorstep. Deal with reputable local firms.

THE SANITARY INSPECTOR TRICK.

A gentleman arrives (always after the husband has gone to work) and introduces himself as a sanitary inspector, and gains admittance by saying that an anonymous letter of complaint has been received regarding the condition of several houses in that particular block.

Then he asks permission to inspect one or two rooms, and creates an impressive atmosphere by tapping walls with a pencil and listening intently with his ear pressed against certain spots.

When an upper room is entered he pretends to have located trouble of some sort, and requests the housewife to go downstairs and tap sharply on the wall immediately below him.

When the " gentleman " has gone, something is usually missing !

ADVICE.—Don't let anybody into your house unless he holds an authority which leaves it without doubt that the visit is genuine. An additional precaution which is most desirable would be to ring up the Clerk to the Local Council and see if everything is all right.

I mention this because, in one case, the householder happened to be acquainted with the local sanitary inspector and challenged the intruder, who calmly remarked : " I am not from the Borough, you know, I have been sent down specially from Whitehall " ; and, if you can believe it possible, the bluff worked !

THE C.O.D. TRICK.

A smart delivery van draws up before a house. One of the messengers in charge arrives with an interesting looking parcel. " Blank Express Delivery Co. 3/- to pay."

The parcel is addressed to the woman's husband and she takes it in, pays the fee and an official looking receipt slip is furnished. When the husband returns the parcel is opened with haste and curiosity, and is found to contain nothing but old rubbish.

ADVICE.—Beware of smart looking men usually wearing a peaked cap and leather satchel. Tell them that your husband is not at home but if they will call again when he is they will be attended to.
You will never see them again.

THE FAMILY BEREAVEMENT TRICK.

An individual calls at a house where there has recently been a death and represents himself as the agent for a firm from whom the deceased has ordered books or other articles. There is hardly any need for him to display his artfully designed order as the state of mind of the relative is such that he or she usually hastens to pay the debt that they imagine was incurred by the dead.

ADVICE.—Ask them to submit in due course any claims they may have against the deceased's estate, when they will be attended to.

THE WIRELESS TRICK.

A man calls on people who have taken houses on a new building estate, mentioning the name of one of the most famous wireless firms, who states that he is Area Superintendent for the district and is making a personal call on new residents to further the firm's business.

Noticing that no aerial is erected he displays attractive literature of wireless sets and very attractive prices and frequently secures an order on the ground that special conditions are being made to those recently installed in new houses. He asks for a small cash payment on account as evidence of the contract. He usually gets it and that is the last you see of him.

ADVICE.—Don't pay out cash deposits until after the goods have been delivered.

THE HOUSEWIVES' PROTECTION RAMP.

Agents are touring London and the suburbs offering protection against unauthorised callers. The Agents point out that it is highly desirable that housewives should make a firm stand against the ever increasing bands of travellers, hawkers, beggars who waste so much of the average housewives' time ; the objectionable habits of the gentleman who puts his foot inside the door and intimidates women into giving alms they can ill spare or buying articles for which they have no need are stressed. Advantages of banding together are pointed out by the agents, and for a membership fee of only 1/- the privileges of legal and police (*sic*) protection is promised. A disc badge, to be fixed to the gate-post, is claimed to be as effective as any Ju-Ju, etc.

ADVICE.—Keep a dog and save your shilling.

THE BOOT REPAIRING SWINDLE.

An ingenious swindler, usually posing as an ex-Service man, calls on housewives offering to repair boots and shoes at a low rate and re-deliver them when the work is done. Neither the boots nor the pedlar are ever seen again.

FOOTBALL CLUB PRIZE.

A man calls and tells the occupant of the house that the son has won £30, but the prize cannot be drawn unless the arrears of subscription are paid.

In one case of which I am aware a woman was induced to part with £2. The caller was never seen again.

LUCKY CHARMS.

An individual arrives at a home peddling these mascots. If he doesn't manage to sell one he solemnly starts cursing the inmates by " bell, book and candle," and reserves a special brand for the children. Such is the credulity and superstition of some people that they fall for it.

ADVICE.—Get hold of the nearest policeman as quickly as possible.

THE KEY TRICK.

A man calls on people who are looking out for houses (the information is usually derived from reading advertisements in public libraries) and brings a key which he says is that of a house which is to let. An order to view is produced and a deposit of 5/- is asked on the key.

Needless to say the key does not fit the house.

CHAPTER II.

PITFALLS OF " HIRE " AND " INSTALMENT " PURCHASES.

I wish to make it clear that I touch on this subject mainly in order that my readers may be able to distinguish between buying a commodity on the hire purchase system, and buying it by instalments.

To avoid legal terms, the difference is this : In a hire-purchase agreement a person contracts to hire the article and to pay so much per month for the hire thereof.

The article remains the property of the firm until the given number of instalments have been paid.

The agreement provides that at the end of that period the article shall become the property of the hirer.

The hirer, therefore, cannot himself dispose of the article during the period of the currency of the hiring unless, before disposal, he pays to the firm the total value of all the instalments which remain unpaid.

It is usual and proper that every hire-purchase agreement should contain a proviso entitling the hirer to return the article and terminate the hire without any further liability, but only after a given number of instalments have been paid.

The question of the number of instalments to be paid before the hirer is entitled to return the article without further liability must depend upon its initial cost, and readers must use their own judgment on this point.

Now, the purchase of commodities by instalments is a totally different matter. Under this system a person contracts to buy a commodity, but to pay for it by instalments.

This is a definite purchase, and the property passes from the seller to the buyer forthwith ; but it is usual for the contract to contain a proviso that the buyer will not dispose of the commodity until he has completed the total instalments due.

There is no question of returning the goods. If the instalments are not kept up the firm concerned has the right to sue in the courts for debt.

The pitfalls in this system are due to the dishonesty, and I use that word advisedly, of the canvassers employed by the firm. They go from door to door, choosing a time when the husband is not at home, inducing the women to commit themselves to colossal expenditure by a trick that takes the form of pretending to supply an article on a month's trial free of cost. The dupe is asked to sign a receipt, which naturally she does, and that receipt is, in fact, a contract to buy an article costing anything up to £25 or £26 by instalments.

ADVICE.—I have written at such great length in the columns of JOHN BULL on this subject that I do not think it necessary to issue any further warning than this. Never put your name to any paper until you have read every word of what you are signing. Never sign anything on the spot. Tell the traveller to leave the paper with you and come back next day when you have had an opportunity of studying it. Show it to your husband and several friends, and get their views. You will probably find that the astute traveller will not return the next day, and that you will never see him again.

CHAPTER III.
EMPLOYMENT AND SPARE-TIME PITFALLS.
EMPLOYMENT WITH INVESTMENT.

One of the most lucrative and popular of modern swindles is the method under which the victim is invited to invest his money by becoming an " area distributor " of some commodity, such as motor oils, greases, accessories, etc., etc.

One of the worst cases of this description which came before me was where over £12,000 was secured from area " concessionaires " who had the exclusive right to sell motor oils within an allotted territory. The oil, of course, was " blended by a fixed and secret formula under a highly technical process demanding the skill of expert chemists." The cost of an area concession ran from £100 to £300, and was described as a " returnable investment." The project was a failure and the unfortunate investors lost all their money.

A similar adventure was started some years ago in regard to the treatment of motor tyres to render them puncture-proof. An American organisation some three years ago attempted a similar scheme by inserting advertisements in our daily papers for a " distributing manager " for a certain commodity connected with motor cars. The manager was to be in charge of the whole of the British Isles, and the correspondence which passed was distinctly amusing and ran as follows :—

" I am submitting your application, *along with several others*, to our Board for final decision as to this very important appointment . . . it is my belief that I am going to be able, following our Board meeting on Thursday, to send you a very welcome and definite statement on the appointment."

My correspondent naturally was given the "appointment," but the letter announcing the good news was hectographed and had obviously been distributed to many others. The only little ceremony connected with the appointment was a request that his acceptance should be cabled together with a sum of £21 for "purchasers' samples"! I was unable to follow the case further because my correspondent naturally shut down, and as far as I am aware never heard again from the American company which was so anxious to capture our markets.

ADVICE.—In all cases like this no one should invest any money or accept any appointment unless there has been a rigid examination of the value of the project and the money behind it. The word "area-distributor" is really only a euphemism for the good old English word "pedlar," sometimes described in the west-country as a "Johnny come fortnight!" It is easy airily, to allot a county to be exploited, but when it comes to a question of selling the goods, it is another story. The area distributor in effect will have to put a pack on his back and stump the country with his wares. It is much better to spend a few pounds on the advice of a Solicitor than to rush blindly into such adventure.

HOME EMPLOYMENT.

Of all the methods of extracting money from people of all ages and both sexes this is undoubtedly the most profitable. Financial stringency and taxation have in many cases made it vital for many people to attempt to supplement their income.

It is only possible to refer in general to this matter as to particularise would necessitate the production of a book as big as a novel. I will endeavour to categorise the subject as briefly as possible under the following headings :—

(a) Manufacture of commodities at home by the aid of apparatus and material sold by the promoters of the scheme.

ADVICE.—When considering any of such projects it is vital to calculate, firstly, whether the finished article will be saleable at all, and, if saleable, whether there will be a market in the vicinity. It is usual for the promoters of the project to guarantee to accept the finished article "if it is up to standard" and it is as well to remember that the judge of what is up to standard is naturally the promoter. I have known of case after case where the finished article has been rejected and there is no remedy. It should be remembered and duly considered before undertaking any home employment that there is always the overwhelming competition of the mass production of highly organised factories, with big capital behind them, able to purchase raw material in the markets of the world at the lowest possible rates. Frankly, I know of no commodity of this description which can be produced at home which has any profitable saleable value.

(b) Home Employment of the "spare time" type.

This embraces a multiplicity of frauds and I will merely indicate types.

Advertisements are inserted for "spare time workers" of either sex and applicants are asked to forward (e.g., 3s. 6d.) for an instruction guide which is stated to be necessary to enable them to understand the working details. The fee brings a miscellaneous packet of rubbishy circulars with alleged mail order schemes.

"Secret" formulæ for boot polishes, home brewing and beauty specifics are part and parcel of these money-making schemes. The ideas are generally of the snowball type, and are calculated and intended to incite and induce an honest fool who has lost his money to endeavour to catch other people and reduce them to the same state of what I frankly describe as dishonesty. It is a horrible maelstrom and takes a strong-minded person to decide that he will not be a party to deceiving his fellow men.

There is then the type of home employment which consists of "courses of instruction." Some years ago an individual who, I am glad to say, eventually ended up in one of His Majesty's prisons was able to induce many people to undergo a course of instruction in producing showcards of a somewhat decorative type by hand. I saw many of the specimens of the handiwork of the unfortunate students. They were crude to a degree and no amount of instruction could ever have trained the majority of the students to geometric drawing, let alone artistic effect. It is hard to believe that people could have been induced to imagine that the untutored human hand could compete with the printing press and the lithograph. However, the business flourished, and even extended, and shortly before the heavy hand of the law descended on the proprietor, unfortunate people (mostly ladies) were being induced to attempt to make gloves (out of materials supplied by the promoter, of course) in competition against machines and mass production.

Another variation is the making of blouses, children's dresses, etc., etc., out of silk and other materials supplied by the promoter. It is the old story every time of the finished article not being "up to standard."

I will conclude with the lowest type of home employment, and that is the addressing of envelopes. There are thousands of people whose labour is sweated to a degree beyond comprehension who burn the midnight oil in this laborious and soul-killing task.   The value of their labours will be evident when I disclose that addresses, or perhaps I should say a list of addresses, is one of the most valuable, if not the most valuable asset, of the home employment pest.   Many of my readers have been surprised to receive a circular and wonder how their address was obtained. There are, of course, such things as postal guides and telephone directories, but I can state *and prove* that addresses are sold at a price of about 10s. per thousand by one firm to another, *but only after the addressee has failed to respond to the various lures and flies which have been dropped over the pool.*   Somebody else then " has a go," and tries a different type of fly, and so the game goes on till at last the fish is hooked by somebody.

Space does not permit me to mention all the types of swindle which fall within the category of home employment.

ADVICE.—The only advice I can give is to view with grave suspicion any offer which seems to be " too good to be true."   Bear in mind especially that where home work necessitates the purchase of material, e.g., silk, wool, leather, tools, apparatus, etc., it may be taken for granted that the main object of the promoter is to sell his material at an outrageous profit with the full intention of never buying the finished article and sheltering behind the unassailable excuse that it is " not up to standard."

CHAPTER IV.

SUSPICIOUS HEALTH CLINICS AND THE DANGERS OF HOME TREATMENT.

There is no matter which brings me a greater flow of enquiries than that relating to organisations which style themselves " Health Clinics," " Health Institutes," etc.   I know that I am approaching a very difficult subject upon which there is a great diversity of opinion, and that is the question of home treatment.

Indeed, I have never ceased attacking these so-called " Clinics " where the proprietor purports to diagnose a particular complaint by post and prescribe treatment. People of this type do not hesitate to attempt to get the biggest price for the treatment they can, but if the potential patient seems reluctant a " special reduced fee " is suggested.   The majority of complaints treated under this system are Deafness and Catarrh.   I have read many of the diagnosis forms which are sent out in question form.   They simply invite answers which are intended to leave no shadow of doubt that the unfortunate person concerned is suffering from Catarrh, which is the cause of a multitude of human ills.   I should imagine that very few people who work amongst the filth and dust of a great city can be free from this annoying complaint, and the low grade petrol which is vomited from the exhaust pipes of lorries and 'buses in the London streets adds to our trouble.

The cruelty of the business is the typewritten letters which are sent in response to the completed diagnosis form.   They are deliberately intended to terrify.   I have before me at the moment a case of a person who is and has been for many years hopelessly and irretrievably deaf.   For reasons which I need not disclose no artificial aid can be of the slightest value, and yet a cure is promised.   I can say at once that nothing but a personal and exhaustive examination by a qualified medical man could secure an accurate diagnosis of this case.   Here is the type of letter which was sent out :—

" Your trouble is due to chronic Catarrh, which has congested the middle ear, blocking the delicate tubes which must be free to ensure perfect hearing.   This type of deafness is progressive, and there is no doubt that if you had left your deafness unattended you might easily have lost what hearing still remains.

" It is unnecessary for me to picture what it would mean to you if you were forced to lead the lonely and miserable life of the stone deaf "—and this unfortunate man is already stone deaf, has been for years, and always will be.   The letter concludes, " I know you do not want to run that risk, so I am going to prescribe a course of special treatment for you. "

Then follows the packets of pellets and pills which are going to effect the " cure." Their intrinsic value is a few pence—indeed, I hazard the opinion that in many cases their value is actually less than the postage upon them.

To Asthma sufferers this is the sort of literature which is broadcast.—

" The second and, in medical eyes, the most serious aspect of Asthma is that although ' Asthma ' never appears on a death certificate as the cause of death, ' Cardiac Trouble ' does, and small wonder.   Next time you have an attack feel your heart thumping during and after the attack ; the strain," etc. —

To those who suffer from Catarrh (and I imagine a very large proportion of the population do so suffer) this is the stock form letter—

" Catarrh is an infectious disease which, once gaining a hold on the system, breaks down the body's reserves and leaves its victims open to attack from deadly complaints such as Bronchial Pneumonia and Consumption.

" I would not be doing my duty to you as an adviser if I did not solemnly point out that you expose your nearest and dearest to infection as long as you leave your Catarrh unchecked, and run great risks where your own life is concerned."

This is the sort of bunkum which comes out of some of these places—

" I am taking it upon myself to make the restoration of health my purpose in life. I am not asking a fee from you because I believe that if I cannot help you in a spirit of good fellowship I cannot be your personal adviser. My motto is ' Spread Sunshine by Giving Happiness.' "

The literature which emanates from these establishments is fantastic, and in some cases there appears a woodcut of an enormous building which is intended to convey the impression that the clinic actually exists and patients are treated therein.

These people depend mostly on advertisements and the post for their victims, but one of their favourite tricks is to descend upon a provincial town and get an advertisement inserted in a provincial paper announcing the arrival of the " famous specialist."

This is the type of advertisement :—

DEAFNESS—MORE AMAZING CURES.
Severest cases still yielding to remarkable new treatment.
NO INSTRUMENTS—NO OPERATIONS.
Famous Specialist resumes Free Consultations.

When the place gets too hot to hold him the " famous specialist " clears out and sets up somewhere else under a similar system. Many of these men, in addition to calling themselves " specialists," add numerous letters after their names, which are intended to create the impression that they hold medical degrees, and there is no question whatever but that they *intend* the public to believe that they are qualified medical men.

ADVICE.—Have nothing whatever to do with any organisation which purports to diagnose by post and to treat ailments affecting vital organs, such as the eye, the ear, throat and nose, etc., etc. The most irretrievable damage may be done. In these days of free treatment at Hospitals, of treatment by qualified medical men under the National Health Insurance Act, etc., there is no excuse whatever for placing your health in the hands of these human vampires who merely want to suck your last penny out of you.

Those who read what I have written may feel inclined to wonder whether or not I am not expressing opinions which should only be given by a medical man. That would be a very fair comment, but those opinions and the advice which I give are the direct result of reading, day in and day out, the pathetic letters which reach me from the victims of the quack who, with their health often further impaired, once more have to seek relief and treatment from qualified medical practitioners.

I do not think that it is generally known that the Medical Act of 1858 was passed " not to prevent unqualified persons from practising, but to enable the public to distinguish between qualified and unqualified practitioners."

It is an offence under the Act for a person to append letters to his name intended to convey the impression that he is a qualified medical man, and it is interesting to remember that persons who are not on the " Medical Register " are not entitled to recover any charges for surgical or medical services—which means to say they cannot sue you in the County Court if you don't choose to pay their bills. Most of them, however, knowing the law, collect their fees in advance, so that the question does not arise !

My frank opinion is that the General Medical Council could do a lot to stop this public evil by prosecuting those harpies who pretend to be qualified but who are not.

CHAPTER V.
BOGUS COMPETITIONS.

During the past five years there has been in this country a perfect spate of competitions for prizes offered by firms selling in drapery, wearing apparel, etc., etc. The idea was imported from America, where apparently it met with great success, and judging by my postbag and the extensive advertising and circularising which is still going on it is doing pretty well here. The competition, so called, takes the form of solving a puzzle, the solution of which is so blatantly manifest that no one in possession of their senses could fail to succeed.

When the solution is submitted to the firm a letter is received by return of post conveying the warm congratulations of the " competition manager " on the success of the entrant. There is one little proviso, however, that is usually overlooked, and it is contained in the following words:—" If you get the correct solution you are expected to patronise and recommend this warehouse. Nothing could be easier or simpler —— " With these last few words I cordially agree, but hundreds and hundreds of people have written to me informing me of their success in *having won the first prize*, and asking me if the scheme is a genuine one. My reply has always been that they will be able to form an opinion on that point if they " patronise " the warehouse and scrutinise the goods which are sent in return for their money.

I can say here that I have on occasions sent, through my agents, wrong solutions, but I have never failed to receive a letter congratulating me on my success in winning the first prize !

The harm I see in bogus competitions of this description is that I have known of many cases where the poorest of the poor have scraped together somehow (frequently by borrowing from neighbours) a sovereign which has been expended in the purchase of goods, because the sender has honestly believed that a prize of £125 will surely follow the transmission of the sovereign.

That prizes are awarded there is no doubt, but the methods under which this is done are not disclosed, although some years ago it was admitted to me by the promoters of one of these competitions that it was a question of the first letters taken out of the box in the morning—in other words the competition was nothing more than a lottery, and therefore illegal, and I did not hesitate to say so in the article I wrote at the time.

I do not make, and have never made, any comment on the value of the goods, but I do condemn most strongly a form of competition which has involved many poor people in a debt of anything from £1 to £2, which it has crippled them to repay and involved them in deprivation and want.

CHAPTER VI.
APPEALS IN THE NAME OF CHARITY.

Charitable appeals fall naturally into three categories :—

(*a*) Genuine.
(*b*) Dubious.
(*c*) Bogus and maybe fraudulent.

To fall within category (*a*) the organisation for which the appeal is made should first of all be of value to the community in its objects, economically administered by voluntary effort as far as possible—that is to say, no commission should be paid to collectors and the salaries paid to the staff should be such as to insure that they are not a drain upon the resources of the organisation. Annual accounts should be properly audited and presented and the reports of the year's work should as far as possible present an adequate picture so that the subscriber may be in a position to form an opinion as to whether his charitable contributions have been well expended.

As to (*b*) there are many charitable appeals where there must be a grave suspicion that the interests of the organisers, from a financial point of view, outweigh their utility to those for whom appeals are made. Too big a paid staff, very few, if any, honorary officials, and a commission on collection should at once warn the public that they should give no subscription without first consulting the Charity Organisation Society, of 296, Vauxhall Bridge Road, S.W.1, who will always, in the strictest confidence, give advice on this subject.

As to (*c*) many charities are started and appeals to the public issued and collections made without any justification whatever. The most outrageous methods are adopted to extract money from the public and very often door to door collectors are employed on purely commission basis.

It should be remembered that people of this description keep within the law as long as the appeals they make are not too definite and they expend a proportion of the money collected on the object in question.

A favourite method of collecting money is to start a " seaside home for children." In one case which came before my notice areas embracing the whole of the London suburbs were covered by collectors who were paid the sum of 5s. in the £ for

" commission " to provide a summer holiday home. There was certainly a holiday home, but the care and accommodation which was afforded to the children was a public disgrace and made it evident that the charity was in the main a means of livelihood for the promoters.

ADVICE IN GENERAL.—If you have the slightest doubt about any charitable appeal, in addition to the Charity Organisation Society there is the British Hospitals Association, which is in a position to recommend whether assistance should or should not be given to appeals of hospitals, clinics, etc., etc.

A final word of warning : Many people of position out of the kindness of their heart, and without sufficient enquiry, lend their name to charitable appeals, only to withdraw them too late when the nature of the appeal is exposed or becomes public. The harm is done as the public have wasted their money and other deserving charities have suffered.

CHAPTER VII.
DUBIOUS FILM COMPANIES.

Advertisements frequently appear in newspapers of the following type : " Lady required ; well educated. Write for interview to —— Film Trust, etc. etc." And again : " Wanted—children and adults with good speaking voices. Clear talking voices essential. Complete tuition given carrying film appearance to suitable applicants. Write for appointment to —— Film Company, etc."

The experience of those who have responded to this type of advertisement will be of value.

Fees running up to £50 are demanded as a matter of course, and various baits are prepared for the unfortunate victim. In one case which was brought to my notice, it was explained to a young lady that if her film voice test in London was successful, she would be given a contract for film work with £5 a week for expenses whether working or not and, in addition, a salary of £3 3s. a day while acting for the film, the film day being one of six hours and all extra work to be paid for at the rate of 5s. an hour.

She paid £2 15s. for the test and was subsequently told that, although her voice was suitable, her pronunciation was not so good. She was then promised lessons in elocution for which a fee of ten guineas was demanded, but she wisely cut her loss and proceeded no further with the adventure.

In another case there was a small boy of some ten years old who had shown some theatrical ability by appearing in an amateur production of a play.

The mother was attracted by the advertisement asking for children with good speaking voices. The boy was taken to London to interview " the manager," and a place was promised for the boy in the next big film produced, provided the film test proved satisfactory. £2 18s. 6d. was demanded and paid. The question of the boy's salary was raised and £12 a week was promised. A fortnight later the mother received a letter saying that, unfortunately, the test had proved that her son was unsuitable for the film that was in contemplation.

In another case a fee of £10 10s. was demanded for training a child for film work. A salary of not less than £1 1s. a day was promised.

Another advertisement ran as follows : " New actors and actresses (all types, including juveniles) for film about to be produced. No fees charged. Salary to be arranged." Answers to the advertisement produced a letter which runs as follows :—

" Our Casting Department has recommended to us your application for a part in our new film." The letter continues to say that " it is impossible to make a definite agreement until a film test is made, the cost of which is, as usual, to be borne by the applicant." In this particular case, about one hundred applicants went through a test at a cost of £1 5s. 0d. per person.

The truth is that fees for film tests are not looked upon with favour by the motion picture industry. When established actors and actresses are unable to get a test the futility of the whole thing will be seen since a film test as carried out by well-known producing companies is a costly business and is only given when a director has carefully considered the applicant's suitability. The entire cost is, of course, borne by the company.

With the present state of unemployment a producer who needs a man or woman to portray a particular character can have his choice of fifty or a hundred experienced artistes at a moment's notice.

ADVICE.—Have nothing to do with any mushroom firms who demand a film test fee as the first step towards employment in an already overcrowded industry ; or with any firm or company which is not engaged in production—that is to say, the company is actually making a film and there are outward and visible signs of that fact.

CHAPTER VIII.
SNOWBALLS.

This is a method of making money which has its attractions. First of all it appears to be within the law, although I doubt it myself; at any rate, as far as I am aware, no prosecutions have ever been launched by the police ; secondly, it makes huge sums of money for its promoters and in some cases a proportionate amount for the participants.

The method is simple and merely consists of inducing your fellow men to pay for the profits you secure for pushing the snowball along. There is one snag, however, and that is that when the snowball comes to rest the last " pusher " is " left to mind the baby."

The commodities sold run from fountain pens, tobacco, cigarettes, pocket books, wallets, notebooks, Treasury note cases, stockings and even apple trees !

Broadly speaking, a commodity is offered for sale at a ridiculously exorbitant price, but if you can induce a certain number of your friends to follow your example you will in effect eventually not only get the commodity for nothing, but a substantial commission as well—in other words, you will have extracted the money from your friends. But they have to do the same thing, and so the snowball rolls along ; but if anybody fails to secure a sufficient number of friends and the chain is broken, the individual concerned is left with a practically useless article for which an exorbitant price has been paid.

I will conclude by recording that in one particular scheme which was extremely successful a lady of some position stated to me that she had made a commission of no less than £400.

It is a merry game, and everybody makes money out of it except the last unfortunate.

CHAPTER IX.
COMMERCIAL AND BUSINESS PITFALLS.
COMPANY FORMATIONS.

In the columns of our daily papers there often appear advertisements pointing out the advantages of converting small businesses into private limited liability companies, and offering to convert and finance them.

A reply to the advertisement usually brings a letter which requests particulars of the business. When these have been furnished no difficulty whatever is experienced in forming the company ! The dupe, indeed, finds it the easiest thing in the world and that it only costs about £49 or less to form a company with a share capital of £2,000. An interview, however, is always requested, and it is at that interview that the spider's web is woven. Assurances are given that the " business is so attractive " that " no difficulty whatever will be experienced " in finding the necessary capital. Indeed, the dupe finds himself put down as a director at a large salary and nothing seems to stand in the way of great developments. Eventually there arrives a formidable array of documents and books, such as Memorandum and Articles of Association, General Minute Book, Register of Members, Share Ledgers, Register of Transfers, Register of Directors, Register of Debentures, lithographed share certificate books, transfer forms, not forgetting " engraved seal fitted to lever press," all for the sum of £49 !

It is not, however, until the dupe enquires when he may expect the cheque for the purchase of the shares which he proposes to issue—in other words, the capital upon which the company has been floated—that he discovers that there is not any capital, and that no capital has ever been guaranteed at all ! He hastily searches through all his correspondence and finds that it is only too true. It is useless for him to suggest that at the interview capital was guaranteed, because that is promptly and emphatically denied and there are no witnesses. The fly is now in the web and is left with a company and the illuminating documents mentioned above, but no capital or the slightest prospect of obtaining any. He has paid £49 for nothing except experience.

Another method employed by these gentry is to get into touch with gentlemen in the provinces to whom very generous terms are offered to act as agents. Their duties are to consist of inserting advertisements of the following type in provincial papers :—

" Tradesmen and shopkeepers, get out of the rut—start branches, form a company and secure all the capital you need. It can be done."

" Are you at a standstill for lack of capital ? Then why not have a limited company ? It only costs a few pounds, but it may bring you in many thousands."

If these advertisements bear fruit the unfortunate gentlemen in the provinces in all innocence produce the victims, and the execution is not long delayed. This is a clever method, because it disguises the identity of the executioner. These people who fleece the public have a very glib vocabulary and a considerable know-ledge of company law—at any rate, sufficient knowledge to keep them out of the criminal courts. They know perfectly well that proceedings for breach of contract against them are too expensive a business to be indulged in. Thus the merry game goes on.

ADVICE.—On no account have any dealings of any nature, except through a solicitor, with people who offer to float a private limited liability company. Make sure that any guarantee to find capital is explicit and that it is backed by tangible assets. On no account let there be any " interview." Let every transaction be in writing. You will find, however, that once you begin to talk about guarantees in writing you will never hear from these gentry again.

ACQUIREMENT OF BUSINESSES.

Closely allied to the above type of swindle and frequently run by the same people is the method of extracting money by purporting to find the necessary capital to acquire a business.

Advertisements are inserted offering to find the necessary money to acquire approved businesses. The victim selects the business he desires and an inspection, valuation and report is carried out by the executioner.

A report is duly sent to the victim, who is asked to complete a letter of acknow-ledgment which is enclosed " should the report be considered satisfactory." The report is naturally considered satisfactory and the *pro forma* letter is signed, and herein lies the ingenuity of the swindle which I will explain a little later on.

The " prospective investor " who was going to find the money to acquire the business begins to get cold feet and, indeed, is inconsiderate enough to " consult his solicitor," and, unfortunately, this solicitor always seems to come to the opinion that he cannot advise his client to put up the money. Furthermore, *most* unfor-tunately, nobody else seems to be anxious to fill the breach.

In the meantime, of course, the victim has paid for the " inspection, valuation and report " and realises too late that he has signed a certificate that he " found the report satisfactory." Of course he did, but the prospective investor has not ! The transaction ends with the victim having paid anything from five to seven guineas for nothing but an extract from the books of the business.

Another method of a somewhat more elaborate nature is to get the victim, in addition to paying for the report and inspection, to effect a policy of insurance as " collateral security " for the promised investment. The victim usually drops anything from £25 to £50 on the deal because the executioner has been cunning enough to produce an insurance policy containing conditions incapable of fulfilment, or because the executioner has promised to take out the policy on behalf of the victim in order to save commission, and when the appointed day arrives the solicitor to the prospective investor discovers that the policy has not been taken out, so there is nothing doing. When the trouble starts the victim realises all too late that it was at the interview that these promises were made and there is no record.

ADVICE.—Similar to that given above.

PARTNERSHIPS.

Advertisements especially appealing to men who have retired from business and saved a little money are carefully and attractively baited. Many, of course, are genuine, but those which appear to be " too good to be true," and almost philanthropic in their aspect, should form the subject of the most rigid scrutiny by a qualified and reputable accountant. *No transaction of any description should take place except through a solicitor.*

I am not proposing to particularise any such cases, but merely to issue a general warning that extreme care should be taken, as there are many pitfalls. It should be remembered that men of straw do not hesitate to enter into contracts they have every intention of breaking, because they know perfectly well that if they are sued in the courts they have no need to worry or even defend as no judgment can be executed against them. Even the office furniture is immune, because it has been acquired on the hire purchase system and is the property of the firm that sold it. Your solicitor will be able to advise you, and it should be taken for granted that in all *bona fide* transactions substantial and tangible assets will be forthcoming to support any guarantees or contracts.

SHARE-PUSHERS.

The sale of worthless or highly-speculative shares provides a lasting means to princely remuneration to a number of plausible but well-educated schemers who, despite all the warnings which have appeared from time to time in "John Bull," still contrive with no small measure of success to capture unsophisticated but moneyed people in all parts of the globe.

I am not exaggerating when I say that, during the past ten years, at least £3,000,000 has been wrung from the British public in the British Isles alone in share swindles of the most blatant type.

In eight leading prosecutions, indeed, more than £250,000 has been involved : and prosecutions have been rare when one takes into consideration the large number of frauds which have been perpetrated without police sequels.

Although the methods employed by share-pushers vary little, and can soon be described, they rely principally on two things. One is literature which has been cunningly worded and elaborately printed. The other is that the actual salesmen —the disciples whose business it is to *sell* the shares by personal contact with the victims—are all picked men, of superior appearance, good bearing, cultured manner, and who have been specially trained to " tell the tale," and to answer convincingly any question that may be put to them.

The chief rogues behind all share-pushing schemes are almost invariably of American origin, or Englishmen who have copied American tactics. When they launch a swindle they first take an office, or offices, in one of the best business centres of London. Then they proceed to obtain from the best available source a list of likely victims—elderly ladies, retired but unsophisticated tradespeople, men and women who have made a habit of gambling in speculative shares, and so on.

The next move is to have extravagant literature printed giving true but dazzling details and figures about any particular industry they are exploiting at the time, and embellished with a lot of untrue material about their own venture. This they send out to their selected clients, quite unsolicited.

At the same time they concoct a bogus newspaper which, got up impressively, and with a real sense of " news " and " production," looks like an ordinary publication. It is given a striking title, like, say, *The Financial Echo*, and most of its well-displayed pages contain financial articles which are absolutely true in every detail. Its contents relate chiefly to first-class companies which, earning big or quite reasonable dividends, make excellent reading.

But, poked away somewhere in these bogus newspapers are untrue but glowing stories about the shares of the company, or companies, which the share-pushers are interested in, and which they take good care is not overlooked by the " clients " they are scheming to dupe.

If the circulars and the inspired " newspaper " (which are mostly circulated *gratis*) are not acknowledged by the " selected " recipient, a series of follow-up circulars are sent in the renewed attempt to make him bite. And once he does bite a smart motor-car generally arrives at his door, and one of the specially trained salesmen descends upon him to thrash home the great possibilities of the deal in question !

Under the combined effect of the literature, the bogus paper, and the superb rhetoric of the inspired caller, the dupe generally is " rushed " into parting with his money, or has handed over valuable securities for transfer into the new proposition, before he realises the nature of the well-laid trap into which he has fallen.

This, then, is the chief method of the share-pushers' stock-in-trade. Sometimes they go even further, and pester unwilling clients with long-distance telephone calls which they suggest have been deemed necessary owing to the fact that, if shares are not snatched up forthwith, the opportunity to get " in " at all will be lost.

Another favourite ruse is to obtain money for shares by promising huge profits within a stipulated time on the understanding that they (the share-pushers) will buy back the shares if their expectations are not fulfilled. Mostly, this stage in their ramifications proves to be the last !

Quite frequently, too, in the midst of the spirited stories travelling salesmen unfold they plant before their deceived victims blank transfer forms which they induce their dupes to sign in ignorance of the fact that they are actually signing away their rights to securities and good shares, that are subsequently sold and the proceeds transferred into " dud " or swindling companies.

ADVICE.—There are several ways to prevent oneself from being robbed by a share-pusher. In the first place never believe anything you read in an unsolicited circular without first taking sound and expert advice. Never pay any attention to the contents of any " newspaper " which emanates from an unknown stock or share dealer without first testing its value independently.

Never listen to a travelling share salesman who arrives in a nice car, or who wants you to sign a paper there and then.

And, above all, ignore telephonic communications, however important they may seem, which come on long-distance wires from " dealers " who, introduced to you for the first time through unsolicited circulars and alleged financial newspapers, want to make you rich quickly.

CHAPTER X.
OUR OLD FRIEND " THE SPANISH PRISONER."

Just as no ornithologist's collection can be deemed to be complete without a specimen of the domestic hen, so can no book of reference relating to deceptions be really informative without a reference to our old and valued friend the Spanish Prisoner ! He is such a hoary headed old sinner that one is almost ashamed to give him space, but he has been going strong for some 50 or 60 years and even now shows no signs of inactivity or decrepitude.

Despite the oft-repeated warnings issued by Scotland Yard he still manages to earn a living, and it is extraordinary to note the number of times readers have written to me to ask my advice. His methods are ingenious and persuasive, and I may say very up-to-date, because he has succeeded in producing most excellent lithographic copies of his shaky handwriting and broken English. He is indeed an unfortunate man because he spends his life in prison in Barcelona. He is fortunate, however, in discovering relatives (distant and otherwise) in this country, and his " only hope of freedom " depends on them ! People all over this country in every walk of life get letters from him, and it is amusing to quote extracts. " My dear relative—although I have not honour of knowing you personally but by hints of my deceased mother he said me belongs to your family and believing you my mother's relative in this I address to you by first time asking your protection for my only daughter Mary of 16 year, etc., etc., —— I am widower and also I am in prison for noble and just political cause and my wish is to name you my daughter's tutor render her to your home to be in your care and protection."

Then follows the story of £50,000 deposited in a bank in England only known to the writer, and which unfortunately he cannot get hold of because of the equally unfortunate fact that he is languishing in a Spanish prison. As some slight recompense for the " care and protection " to be afforded to the daughter a quarter of the sum is promised. There are difficulties, however, which are inherent in every prison, so a suggestion is made that a communication be addressed to a Spanish gentleman who is a trusted friend and who will be in a position to " give facilities." There is not much time to spare as the prisoner's health is far from good.

Other variations take the form of thousands of bank notes deposited in a railway station in France, and other parts of the Continent conveniently distant.

If the dupe falls by replying to the letter the next act in the comedy is staged. One of the warders has a brother-in-law and the warder is a kindly man much in sympathy with the unfortunate political prisoner (sometimes he is a bankrupt through no fault of his own) and out of the kindness of their hearts the warder and the brother-in-law " get going."

To make a long story short the dupe eventually parts with money, sometimes large sums, which is necessary as a preliminary to the recovery of the deposit in the Bank, the bank notes in the trunk or the securities in the " secret pocket " of the overcoat " inadvertently left " in some inaccessible place.

It is not necessary for me to do more than briefly indicate the methods by which this fraud is perpetrated. It may be wondered why the Spanish Authorities do not proceed, but it will be realised how difficult it is to secure the necessary evidence.

I have always been puzzled by the method which the " prisoner " adopts in settling on whom he should write to. Perhaps some day, For Auld Lang Syne, he will enlighten me !

Printed in Great Britain and Published by ODHAMS PRESS LTD., Long Acre, London, W.C.2